CONTENTS

LEX LUTHOR
SUPERMAN'S GREATEST ENEMY

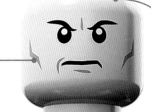

A serious face as
Lex plots Superman's
downfall

No need for a
hairpiece with
this famously
bald villain

A sharp business suit
to wear to work at his
company – LexCorp

EVIL GENIUS

A master inventor, Lex Luthor
designed and built a Kryptonite-
powered battle armour to defeat
Superman once and for all. The
bait in his trap? None other than
Wonder Woman herself!

The Lex Luthor minifigure
was the first LEGO® DC Comics
Super Heroes villain not to come
from Batman's rogues gallery.
Instead, powerful billionaire Lex
Luthor is Superman's arch nemesis
in the city of Metropolis.

POWER ARMOUR

LEX LUTHOR'S MEAN, GREEN MACHINE

VITAL STATS

OWNER: Lex Luthor
USED FOR: Setting a trap for Superman
GEAR: Kryptonite gun

SET NAME: Superman vs Power Armour Lex
SET NUMBER: 6862
YEAR: 2012

Pipe connects gun to armour
Clear dome protects control seat
Long gun barrel channels Kryptonite energy
Wonder Woman is held in Lex's clutches!
Flexible joints allow for giant strides

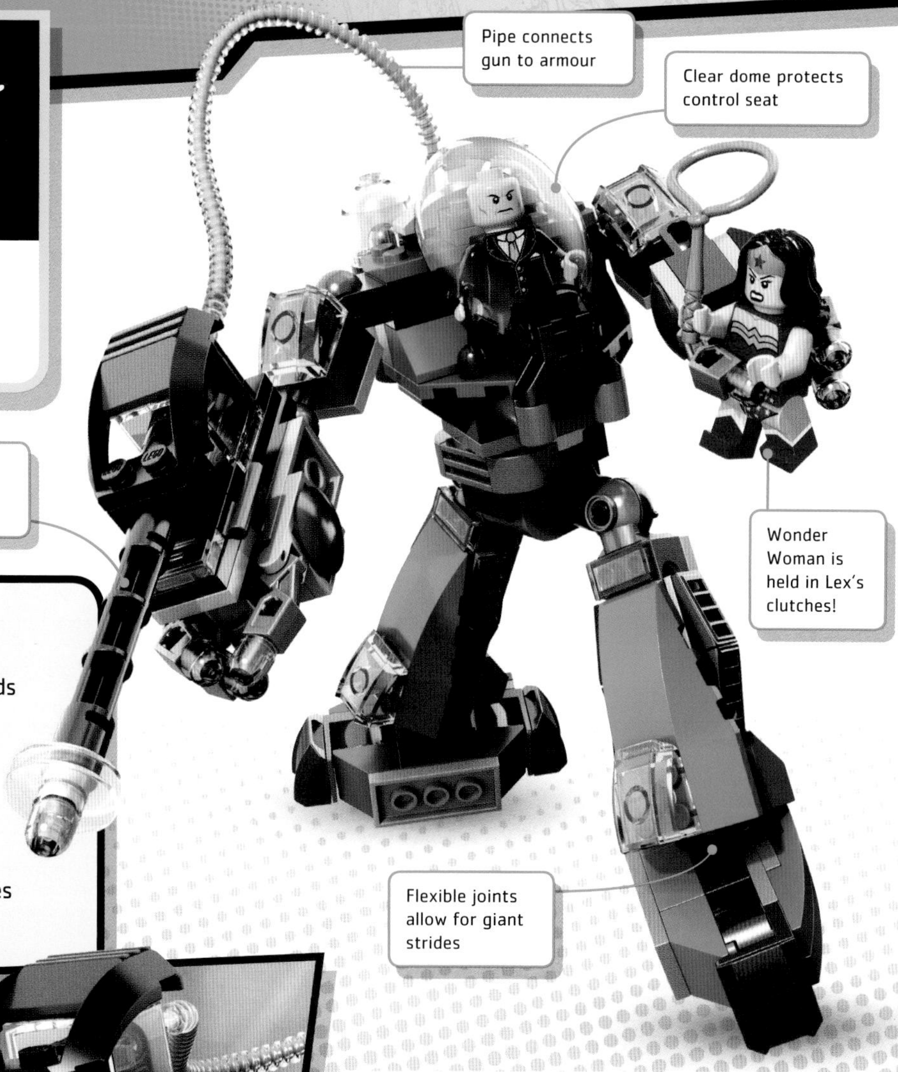

ALL FINGERS AND THUMBS

A LEGO® Technic pin holds the gun in place on the armour's right arm. Both hands have moveable thumbs and two moveable fingers that can grasp minifigures and other objects.

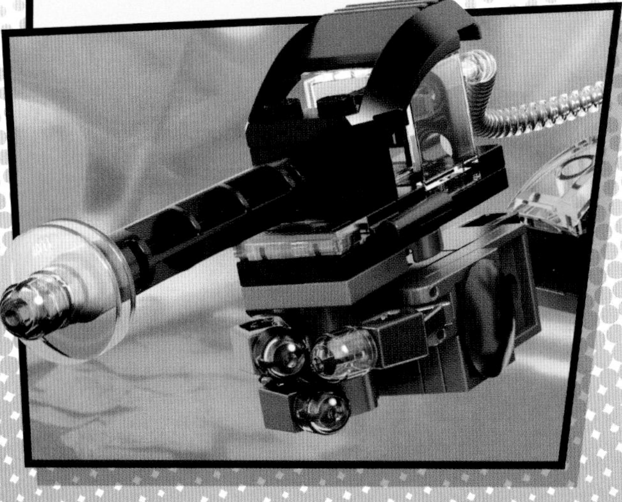

Lex Luthor moved one big, mechanical step closer to catching Superman with this Kryptonite-powered robo-suit. Holding Wonder Woman prisoner, he plans to lure Superman into a trap and blast him with the mech's Kryptonite gun.

LEX LUTHOR'S MECH
Superman vs Power Armour Mech (set 6862) allowed Lex Luthor to show off his technology skills in a big, green fighting machine. LEGO Technic pins in the right arm turn his gun as he takes on two Super Heroes at once.

LEX LUTHOR
WICKED WARSUIT

VITAL STATS
....

LIKES: Kryptonite
DISLIKES: Red-caped heroes
FRIENDS: None
FOES: Superman
SKILLS: Great intelligence
GEAR: The Deconstructor

SET NAME: Lex Luthor (polybag)
SET NUMBER: 30164
YEAR: 2012

This Luthor variant has a snarling face.

The warsuit follows Luthor's classic comic-book green and purple colour-scheme.

Rocket packs allow Lex to fly like Superman

Remove the warsuit and you'll see a power-pack printed on the minifigure's chest.

FEAR THE DECONSTRUCTOR!
One of Luthor's most despicable weapons, the Deconstructor can pull apart any LEGO object made of black bricks. Luckily Superman's costume is blue and red. Phew!

DID YOU KNOW?
This exclusive Lex was given away at GameStop stores with pre-orders of LEGO® Batman™ 2: DC Super Heroes.

Realising that he was physically no match for Superman, Lex designed a powerful new armour, capable of flight and boosting his strength to super-human levels. He really will do anything to bring down the Man of Steel.

BIZARRO
SUPERMAN IN REVERSE

PROPERTY OF MERTHYR TYDFIL PUBLIC LIBRARIES

VITAL STATS
....

LIKES: Being bad
DISLIKES: Clark Kent
FRIENDS: The Bizarro League
FOES: Superman
SKILLS: Freezing vision and flaming breath
GEAR: Purple-blue flying cape

SET NAME: Bizarro
SET NUMBER: COMCON022
YEAR: 2012

DID YOU KNOW?
In LEGO® Batman™ 3: Beyond Gotham Bizarro stole Luthor's duplication ray to make Bizarro versions of the Justice League.

Chalk white and wrinkled skin

Reversed S-shield and muted colours

A medallion made of rock helps Bizarro remember his own name.

BIZARRO BOTHER
The other side of Bizarro's head shows an even angrier face. The mixed-up minifigure was a San Diego Comic-Con exclusive, only available at the convention.

Created by evil genius Lex Luthor, this muddled clone of Superman gets everything the wrong way around. Childish and prone to throwing tantrums, Bizarro sees life in reverse. For him, good is bad and bad is good.

GENERAL ZOD
KRYPTONIAN CRIMINAL

VITAL STATS

LIKES: Making war
DISLIKES: The Phantom Zone
FRIENDS: Faora
FOES: Superman, Jor-El
SKILLS: Super-strength and speed
GEAR: Kryptonian helmet

SET NAMES: Superman: Battle of Smallville, Superman: Black Zero Escape
SET NUMBERS: 76003, 76009
YEAR: 2013

DID YOU KNOW?
A General Zod minifigure without his cape and helmet is available in Superman: Metropolis Showdown (set 76002).

Two-sided head featuring heat-vision eyes on the reverse

Black cape

General Zod's Kryptonian emblem

SPACE ARMOUR
Following Superman across the galaxy, Zod needs a Kryptonian battle helmet to breathe Earth's atmosphere. The aliens first clashed in the small town where Clark Kent, aka Superman, grew up – Smallville.

As the Planet Krypton ripped itself apart, Zod tried to overthrow the Kryptonian council and take control. Defeated, he and his co-conspirators were trapped in the Phantom Zone for all eternity – until Krypton's eventual destruction set them free!

FAORA
ZOD'S SECOND-IN-COMMAND

Faora also shares hair with Nightwing and Beast Boy.

Shock! Faora shares a two-sided head with Wonder Woman!

Faora's family crest

SOLAR-POWERED

Like Zod, Faora needs breathing apparatus to survive Earth's atmosphere, but she soon discovers that the solar system's yellow sun grants her new superpowers of her own. She won't be needing her gun!

Hips printed on the minifigure's body

To save Earth, Superman surrendered himself to Zod. The triumphant General sent his second in command, Faora, to collect the Man of Steel and Lois Lane. Their encounter would lead to a devastating battle in Smallville.

TOR-AN
KRYPTONIAN SOLDIER

VITAL STATS

LIKES: Fighting
DISLIKES: The Phantom Zone
FRIENDS: General Zod, Faora
FOES: Superman,
Colonel Hardy
SKILLS: Piloting the dropship
GEAR: Kryptonian gun

SET NAME: Superman: Battle of Smallville
SET NUMBER: 76003
YEAR: 2013

DID YOU KNOW?
This minifigure has brown hair, just like his comic-book counterpart.

This minifigure has the same head as Lex Luthor.

Tor-An's Kryptonian emblem

No cape for this pilot—it would only restrict his space in the cockpit.

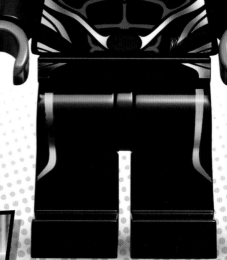

TOO BAD, TOR-AN
As the pilot of the dropship, Tor-An sees all of the action from his domed cockpit. After the battle on Earth, he is banished to the Phantom Zone by Colonel Hardy.

Tor-An helped General Zod track Superman's path through the cosmos to Earth. Genetically engineered to be a soldier and a loyal member of the Kryptonian Warrior Guild, Tor-An is a master of several alien martial arts.

BLACK ZERO DROPSHIP
ALIEN ATTACK CRAFT

VITAL STATS
....

OWNER: General Zod
USED FOR: Swooping down
on unsuspecting planets
GEAR: Missiles,
rotating cannon

SET NAMES: Superman:
Battle of Smallville
SET NUMBERS: 76003
YEARS: 2013

Storage bays
open to reveal
weapons racks

Adjustable fins
aid flight in
atmosphere

Spring-loaded
missiles hidden
within hull

Rotating cannon
fires crackling
energy bolts

DROPPED SHIP
The Dropship is designed to
land on planets, and its fins can
fold down to become feet that
keep the weapons array raised
above the ground.

Criminal Kryptonians General
Zod, Faora and Tor-An set out to
destroy the town of Smallville in
this superpowered spaceship! Only
Superman can stop them, but he will
have to dodge giant missiles and
blasts of alien energy to do so!

13

SMALLVILLE ATTACK
Superman faces new alien foes in
Superman: Battle over Smallville
(set 76003) in a new costume
design to resemble his look from
the 2013 *Man of Steel* movie.

THIS IS "HARDY"
A WALK IN THE
PARK, HARDY
HAR HAR!

SINESTRO
FALLEN LANTERN

VITAL STATS

LIKES: Absolute power
DISLIKES: Hal Jordan
FRIENDS: The Sinestro Corps
FOES: Green Lantern, Batman
SKILLS: Lantern-napping
GEAR: Power staff

SET NAME: Green Lantern vs Sinestro
SET NUMBER: 76025
YEAR: 2015

Double-sided head with a snarling face on the back

Uniquely bright pink face

Symbol of the Sinestro Corps

Yellow and black printing continues on the back of the minifigure.

LANTERN LIFT-OFF
Sinestro stole Hal Jordan's Lantern and placed it within a protective cage on his home planet of Korugar. It has just enough space for one object – either the Lantern or Sinestro himself!

Once considered the greatest Green Lantern of them all, Sinestro was actually using his great powers to enslave alien races. Stripped of his power ring, Sinestro formed the evil Sinestro Corps and became the Green Lantern's sworn enemy.

CAPTAIN COLD
HOODED HOODLUM

VITAL STATS

LIKES: Cold
DISLIKES: Heat
FRIENDS: Gorilla Grodd
FOES: The Flash, Batman,
Wonder Woman
SKILLS: Turning down
the heat
GEAR: Ice shooter

SET NAME: Gorilla Grodd
Goes Bananas
SET NUMBER: 76026
YEAR: 2015

Protective
hood

Coolly
confident
grin

Warm parka
printing on
both sides of
the minifigure

CHILLED TO THE BONE

Captain Cold's alternate face
shows his features frozen
into a frown. Perhaps facing
the Batman wasn't the best
idea – after all, the Caped
Crusader has plenty of icy
experience with Mr Freeze!

When crook Leonard Snart
was captured by The Flash, the
embarrassed villain swore he'd get
revenge. Using his cool intellect
Snart created a chilling gun that
could freeze anyone in their tracks,
including the super-speedy Flash!

GORILLA GRODD
GOING APE

VITAL STATS

LIKES: Bananas
DISLIKES: Rotten fruit
FRIENDS: Captain Cold
FOES: The Flash, Batman, Wonder Woman
SKILLS: Mind control
GEAR: Banana

SET NAME: Gorilla Grodd Goes Bananas
SET NUMBER: 76026
YEAR: 2015

Mind control equipment

DID YOU KNOW?
Gorilla Grodd made his comic debut in issue 106 of *The Flash* back in 1959.

JUST BANANAS
If there's one thing Gorilla Grodd loves, it's trying to take over the world. But if there's another thing he loves, it's nice tasty bananas. So much so that he attacks this unsuspecting truck driver.

Once Grodd was just another gorilla living in a rainforest. That was until a crashed alien spacecraft gave the great ape hyper-intelligence. Now Grodd is able to telepathically control minds!

SEA SAUCER
FISH DISH

Propeller keeps sub moving

The cockpit even has room for a minifigure with a big helmet!

Torpedo launcher

MEGA BITE

Think sharks are scary? Wait until you see this roboshark! Armed with laser shooters on both sides, the swimming cyborg is controlled by Black Manta from inside his Sea Saucer.

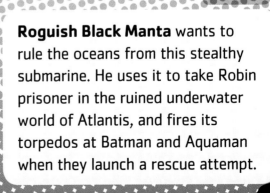

Black Manta symbol

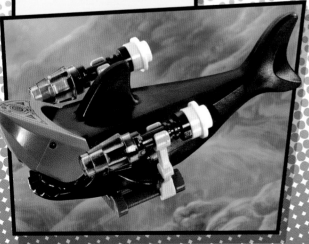

Roguish Black Manta wants to rule the oceans from this stealthy submarine. He uses it to take Robin prisoner in the ruined underwater world of Atlantis, and fires its torpedos at Batman and Aquaman when they launch a rescue attempt.

BLACK MANTA
DEEP-SEA DANGER

VITAL STATS
....

LIKES: Fishing
DISLIKES: The sea
FRIENDS: None
FOES: Aquaman, Batman
SKILLS: Deep-sea diving
GEAR: Spear, Torpedo-toting robo-shark

SET NAME: Black Manta Deep Sea Strike
SET NUMBER: 76027
YEAR: 2015

There's no minifigure head beneath that oversized helmet.

Tubes take air into the helmet

SUPER SUIT

Although Black Manta has no superpowers, he's a formidable foe. His custom-made scuba suit can survive the extreme pressure of the seabed, fire lasers from his eyes, and shoot electric bolts. He's also armed with a spear for closer attacks.

Scuba suit printing continues on the back

The heavy helmet-wearing Black Manta wants to plunge the ocean's depths for treasure and won't rest until he rules the underwater world for himself. The mysterious villain views Aquaman as his enemy, along with anyone who sides with him.

DARKSEID
OVERSIZED ALIEN OVERLORD

VITAL STATS

LIKES: Conquering
DISLIKES: Justice League
FRIENDS: None
FOES: Superman, Cyborg, Green Arrow, Hawkman
SKILLS: Invading planets
GEAR: Hover Destroyer

SET NAMES: Darkseid Invasion
SET NUMBERS: 76028
YEARS: 2015

Cracked grey skin

Darkseid's red eyes can launch laser beams.

Huge gripping hand

CANNONBALL CHAOS

Darkseid's invasion starts in Metropolis, when the alien overlord plays skittles with skyscrapers, blasting cannonballs from a Hover Launcher enlarged for his oversized form.

The tyrannical ruler of Apokolips has set his eyes on the rest of the universe. Invulnerable to anything but his own eye-beams, Darkseid is super-strong and resourceful. Nothing will stop his takeover plans.

HOVER DESTROYER
DARKSEID'S HOVERBOARD

VITAL STATS

OWNER: Darkseid
USED FOR: Fighting flying Super Heroes
GEAR: Omega cannon

SET NAMES: Darkseid Invasion
SET NUMBERS: 76028
YEARS: 2015

Large levers for Darkseid's huge hands

Bright red balls of Omega energy are launched from this cannon.

Space to store second cannonball behind launcher

BALANCING ACT
Darkseid positions his brawny bulk at the back of the Hover Destroyer, standing on special footholds. From this secure stance he takes on a full cohort of Superman, Green Arrow, Cyborg and Hawkman.

Omega symbol on front of craft

Darkseid can match Superman with many alien powers, but one thing that he can't do is fly! It takes three anti-gravity discs to lift the muscular monster on this floating weapons platform, along with his heavy, high-tech cannon.

BRAINIAC
LIVING COMPUTER

VITAL STATS
....

LIKES: Knowledge
DISLIKES: Kryptonite
FRIENDS: Gorilla Grodd
FOES: Superman, Supergirl,
Martian Manhunter
SKILLS: Genius-level intellect
GEAR: Skull Ship

SET NAME: Brainiac Attack
SET NUMBER: 76040
YEAR: 2015

Computer connections

Purple wiring printed on both sides of minifigure

Lime green hands

DID YOU KNOW?
Brainiac even turned Supergirl's dad into a cyborg, for the crime of being a native of Kandor City.

KANDOR CAPER
Brainiac has clashed with Superman on numerous occasions, ever since the Man of Steel discovered that the alien android had shrunk the Kryptonian city of Kandor.

An alien supercomputer from the planet Colu, Brainiac believes that knowledge is power. In order to understand other races he steals entire cities, shrinking them to fit into jars – usually without asking the inhabitants first.

SKULL SHIP
A HEAD FOR HEIGHTS

VITAL STATS
....

OWNER: Brainiac
USED FOR: Invading Earth
GEAR: Cannons, tentacles

SET NAME: Brainiac Attack
SET NUMBER: 76040
YEAR: 2015

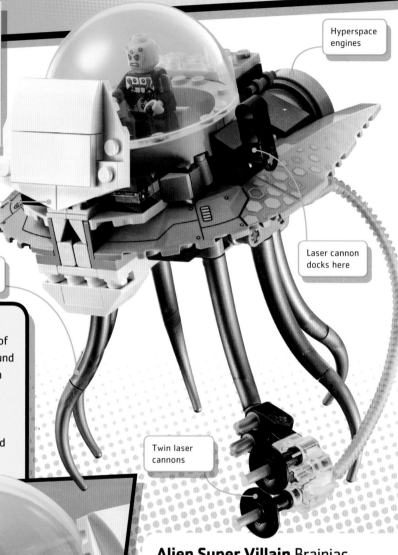

Hyperspace engines

Scary skull face

Laser cannon docks here

Terrifying tentacles!

Twin laser cannons

DOME ALONE
The transparent green dome of Brainiac's Skull Ship is not found in any other LEGO set, though a trans-clear version is used in two LEGO® Space Alien Conquest sets from 2011: UFO Abduction (set 7052) and Alien Mothership (set 7065).

Alien Super Villain Brainiac controls his scary Skull Ship with the power of his mind. He can cause chaos with its two laser cannons and six twisty tentacles, and gets a 360-degree view of the action from its grisly green protective dome.

24

TRICKSTER
PRANKS A LOT!

VITAL STATS
....

LIKES: Tricking people
DISLIKES: Being tricked
FRIENDS: Captain Cold
FOES: The Flash
SKILLS: Telling jokes
GEAR: Anti-gravity boots

SET NAMES: LEGO® DC™
*Comics Super Heroes Justice
League: Attack of the Legion
of Doom!* DVD movie
YEARS: 2015

Two-colour
arms suggest
T-shirt sleeves

No other LEGO
minifigure has
hair this colour

Belt and braces
lined with gadget
pouches

REAR-AXEL

The Trickster's belt and braces
printing continues on his back,
adding more pouches in which
he can store twisted trick items
such as itching powder and
exploding rubber chickens!

Chequered
pattern
continues on
side of legs

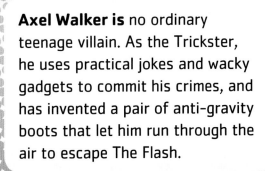

Axel Walker is no ordinary
teenage villain. As the Trickster,
he uses practical jokes and wacky
gadgets to commit his crimes, and
has invented a pair of anti-gravity
boots that let him run through the
air to escape The Flash.

LEX LUTHOR
LEXCORP LEADER

Unusually, this Lex minifigure has locks!

HAIR RAISER
This LexCorp helicopter has eight Kryptonite missiles to launch against Superman – but Lex can't stop Wonder Woman coming to rescue Lois.

Smart-casual sand-coloured clothes of a tech company boss

Lex luxuriates in long hair and a leisure suit for his latest, laid-back look. There's nothing relaxed about his grimace and gun however, which he uses to menace Lois Lane. Perhaps he knows he's still bald under that LEGO hair piece!

LEXCORP HENCHMAN
GRIZZLED GUARD

VITAL STATS
....

LIKES: LexCorp staff benefits
DISLIKES: Not getting to drive the forklift truck
FRIENDS: Other henchmen
FOES: Batman, Superman
SKILLS: Guarding things
GEAR: Bazooka

SET NAMES: Kryptonite Interception
SET NUMBERS: 76045
YEARS: 2016

LexCorp ID badge

Black gloves for doing dirty work

Stud-shooting bazooka rifle

BADDIE BUDDY
The henchman's pal wears the same uniform and a similar scowl, but is clean-shaven. Together they guard a secret stash of LexCorp Kryptonite.

LEXCORP

A henchman needs an impressive resumé to work at LexCorp, and this bearded baddie lists guard duty and bazooka skills among his many talents. In return for loyalty to Lex, he gets a smart green uniform and access to hi-tech weapons.

Project Editor Emma Grange
Editors Tina Jindal, Matt Jones, Ellie Barton,
Clare Millar, Rosie Peet
Senior Designers Nathan Martin, Mark Penfound,
David McDonald
Designers Karan Chaudhary, Stefan Georgiou
Pre-Production Producer Kavita Varma
Senior Producer Lloyd Robertson
Managing Editors Paula Regan,
Chitra Subramanyam
Design Managers Neha Ahuja, Guy Harvey
Creative Manager Sarah Harland
Art Director Lisa Lanzarini
Publisher Julie Ferris
Publishing Director Simon Beecroft

Additional Photography Markos Chouris,
Christopher Chouris, Gary Ombler

First published in Great Britain in 2016
by Dorling Kindersley Limited
80 Strand, London, WC2R 0RL

001–298875–Jul/16

Contains content previously published in LEGO® DC COMICS
SUPER HEROES *Character Encyclopedia* (2016)

Page design copyright © 2016 Dorling Kindersley Limited
A Penguin Random House Company

A CIP catalogue record for this book
is available from the British Library.

ISBN: 978-0-2412-9289-1

Printed and bound in China

www.LEGO.com
www.dk.com
A WORLD OF IDEAS:
SEE ALL THERE IS TO KNOW

ACKNOWLEDGMENTS

DK would like to thank Randi Sørensen,
Paul Hansford, Martin Leighton Lindhardt, Maria
Bloksgaard Markussen, Adam Corbally, Daniel
Mckenna, Casper Glahder, Adam Siegmund Grabowski,
John Cuppage, Justin Ramsden, Karl Oskar Jonas
Norlen, Marcos Bessa, Sally Aston, Sven Robin Kahl
and Mauricio Bedolla at the LEGO Group; Ben Harper,
Thomas Zellers and Melanie Swartz at Warner Bros.;
Cavan Scott and Simon Hugo for their writing
and Sam Bartlett for design assistance.